MIND-TWISTING MAZES

Complete the puzzles, then colour them in!

Over 80 fiendish **MAZES** to bamboozle

D0318343

MIND-TWISTING MAZES

Complete the puzzles, then colour them in!

CARLTON KIDS

THIS IS A CARLTON BOOK

Puzzles copyright © British Mensa Limited 1994

Text and design copyright © Carlton Books Limited 2016

Editor: Tasha Percy
Designer: Rachel Lawston
Art Editor: Dani Lurie
Production: Lisa Cook

Published in 2016 by Carlton Books Ltd
An imprint of the Carlton Publishing Group
20 Mortimer Street, London W1T 3JW

10 9 8 7 6 5 4 3 2 1

A catalogue record for this book is available from the British Library.

ISBN: 978-1-78312-207-3

Printed in China

WELCOME to this book of mind-twisting mazes. The pages that lie ahead are filled with patterns and images containing a pathway that will take you on a journey with every twist and turn. The magic of the maze means there is a reward to be had with each one – the satisfaction of solving the riddle and finishing your journey!

So let your brain boggle as you work your way from the green dot at the start of the maze and aim for the finish flag at the end. Some of the mazes may have more than one starting point so you'll need to figure out which one leads to the finish. You'll have to use all your intelligence to navigate the route as these mazes are fiendishly hard. Enjoy the patterns and hidden pictures from different cultures – you can colour them in as you go, or once you've completed the mazes!

Fancy more of a challenge? Why not time yourself and see which maze you can complete the quickest? But if you get really stuck along the way to the checkered finish flag, then it's fine to allow yourself a quick glance at the answers at the back of the book.

The thrill of navigating a complex puzzle is what makes these mazes so fascinating, so if you like this book you'll enjoy Mensa Kids. You can join the society and enjoy solving many more puzzles. For more information write to:

British Mensa Ltd
St John's House
St John's Square
Wolverhampton
WV2 4AH
UK

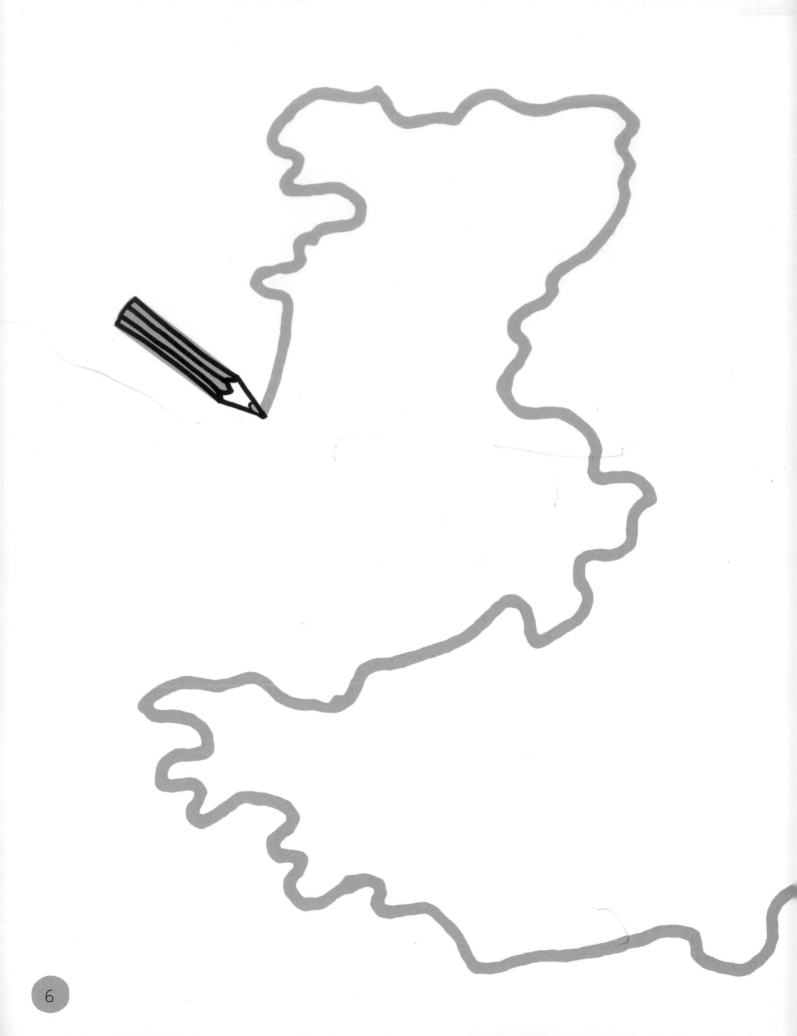

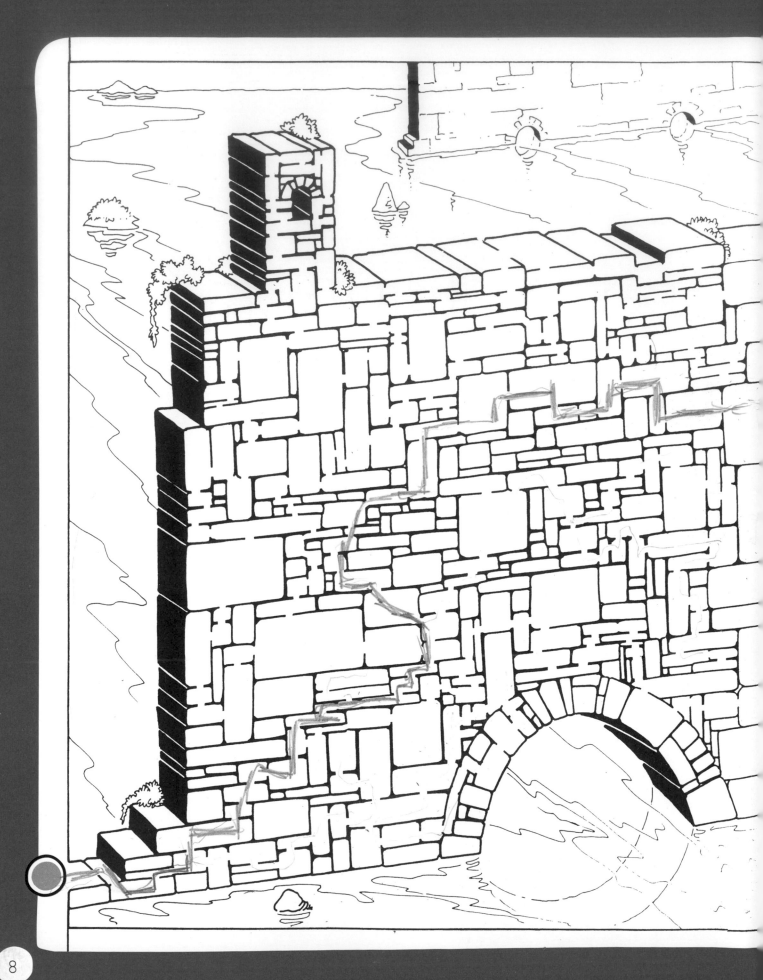

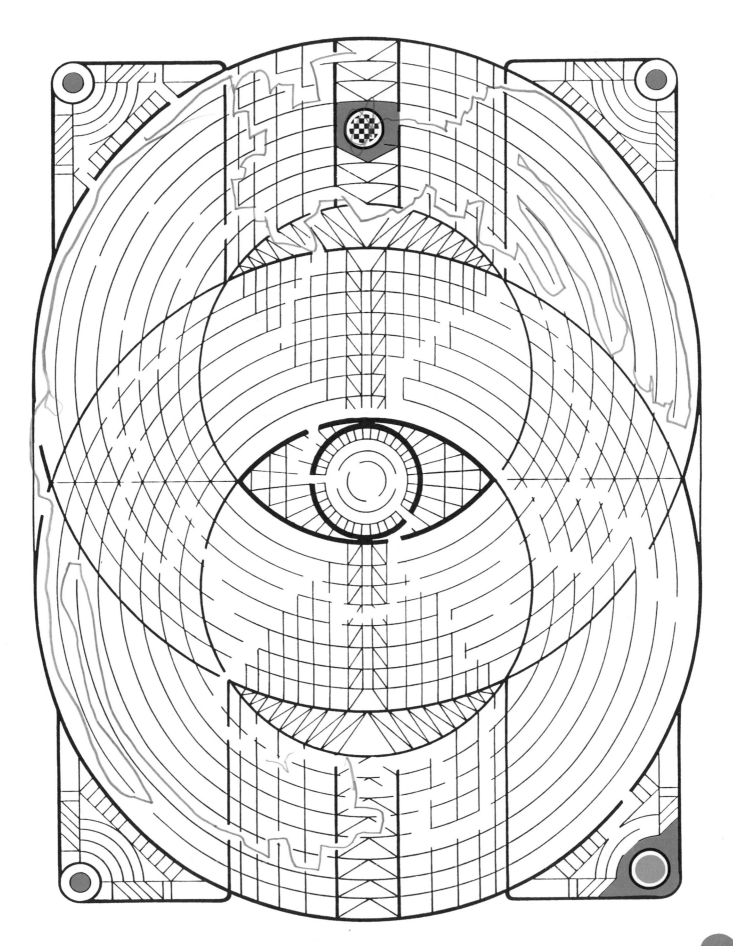

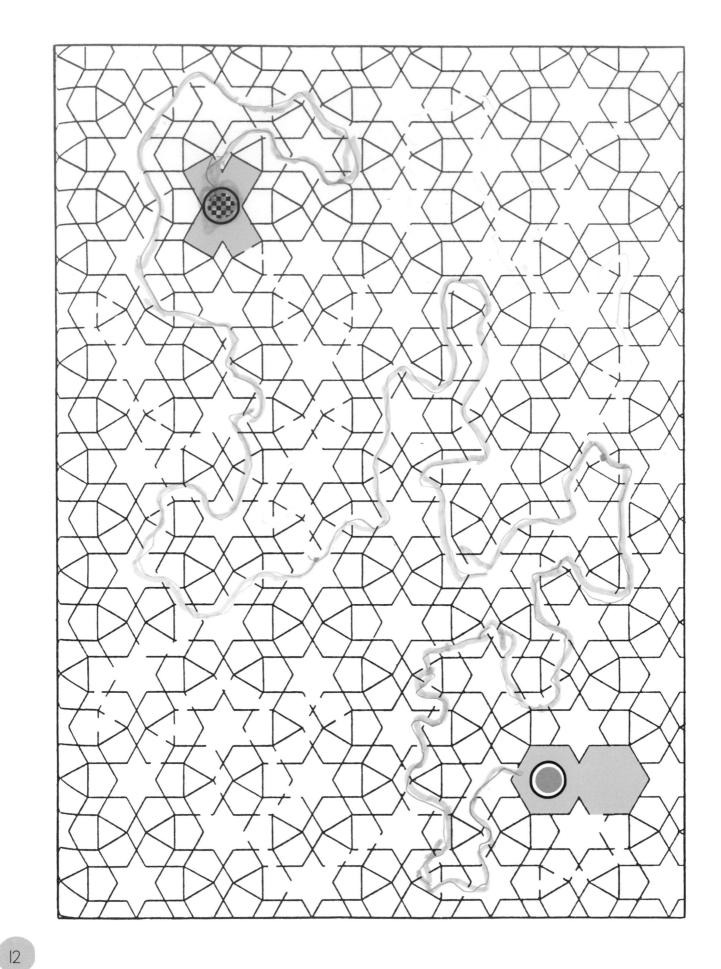

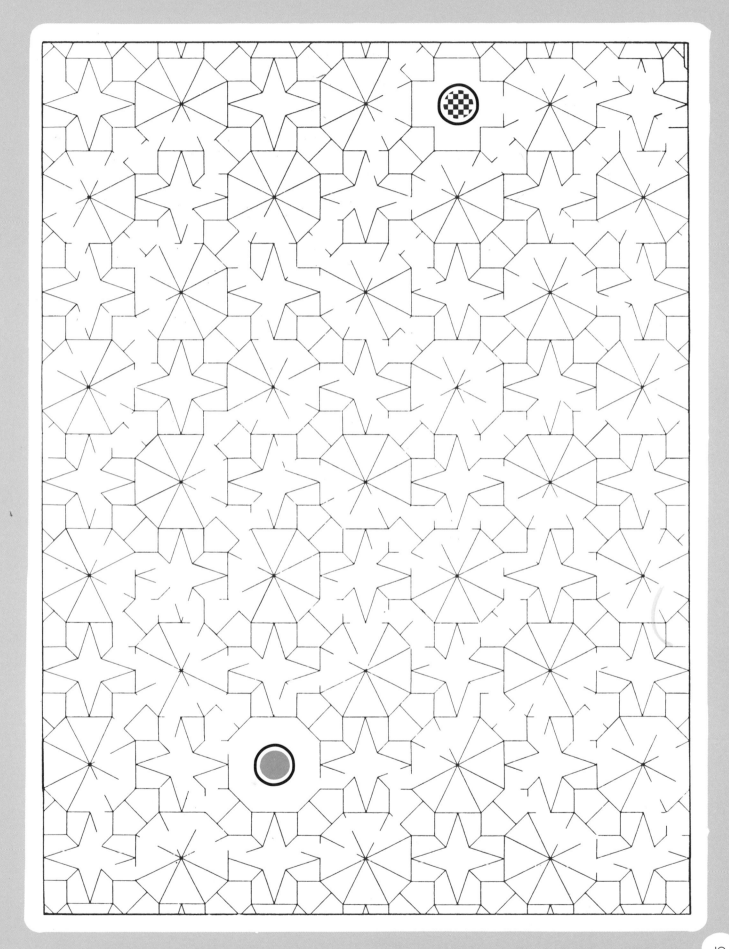

13

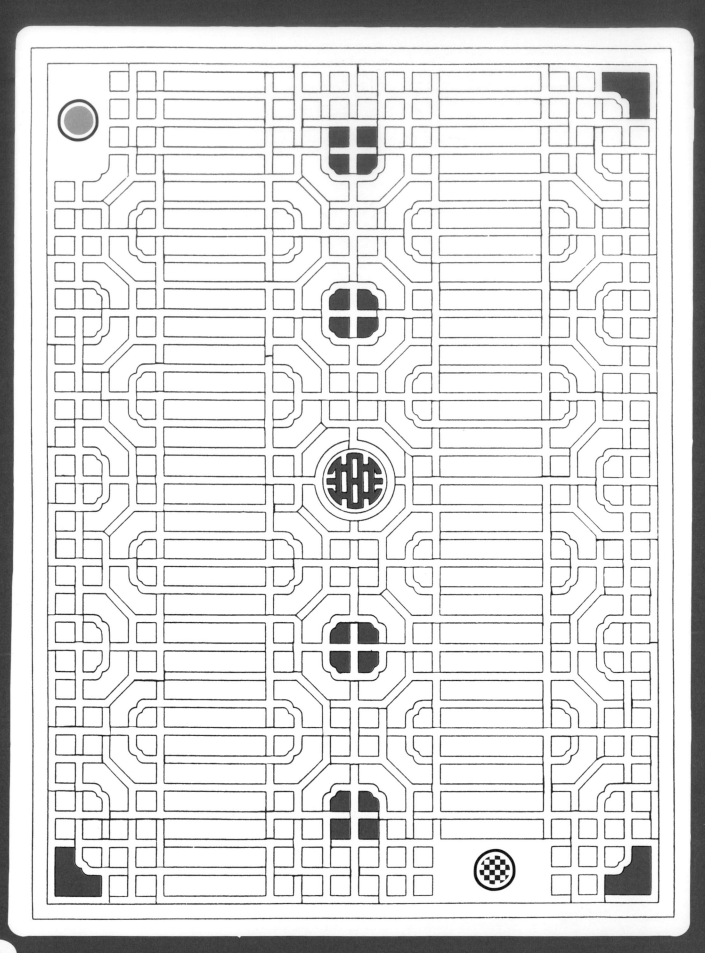

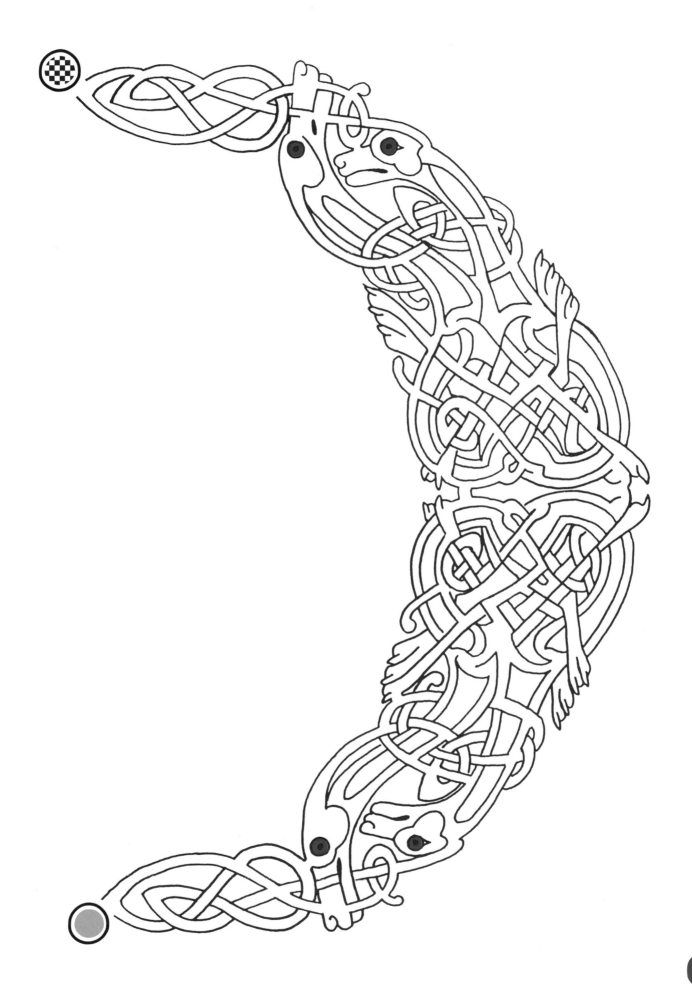

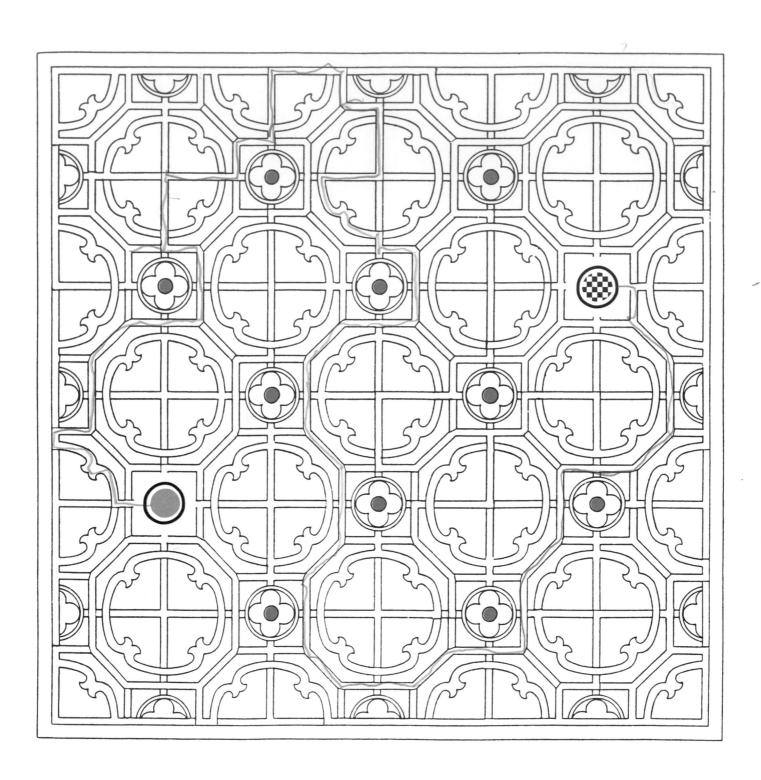

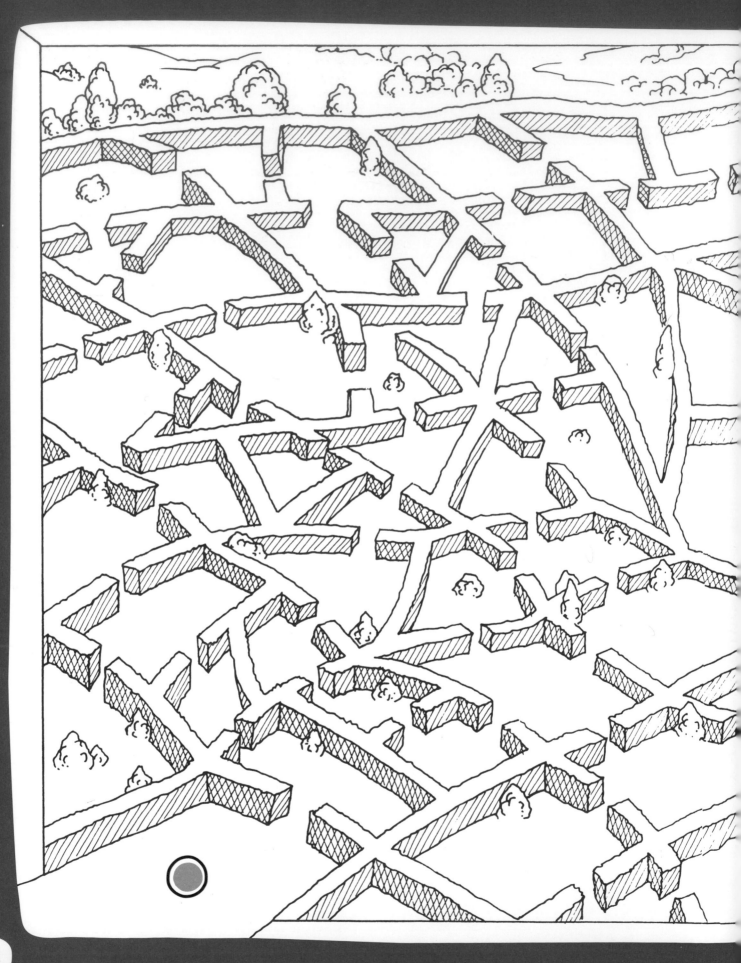

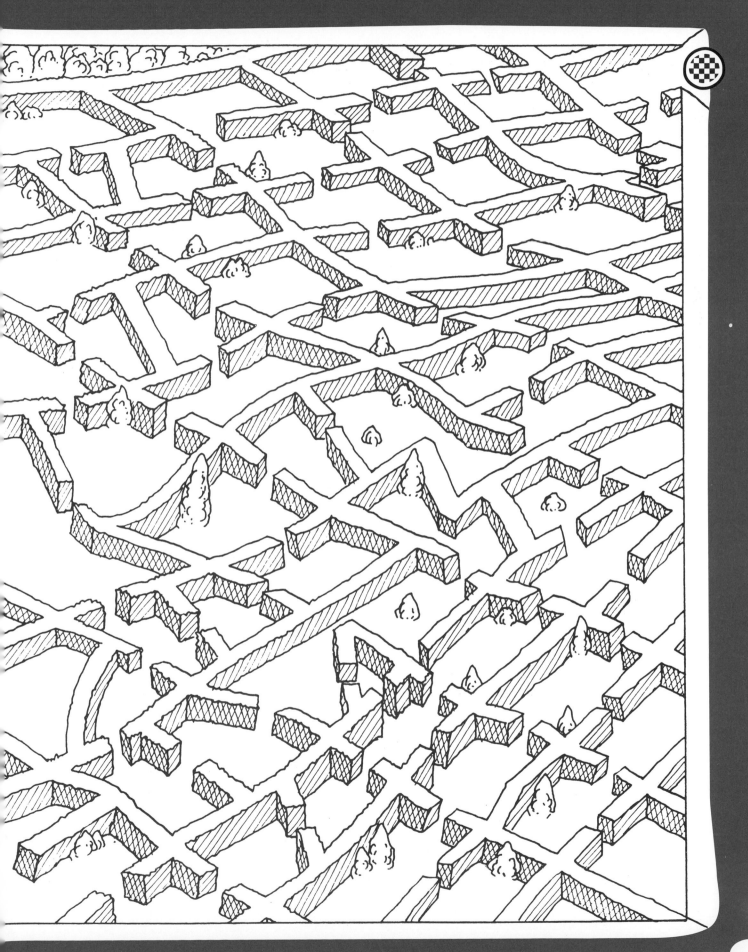

29

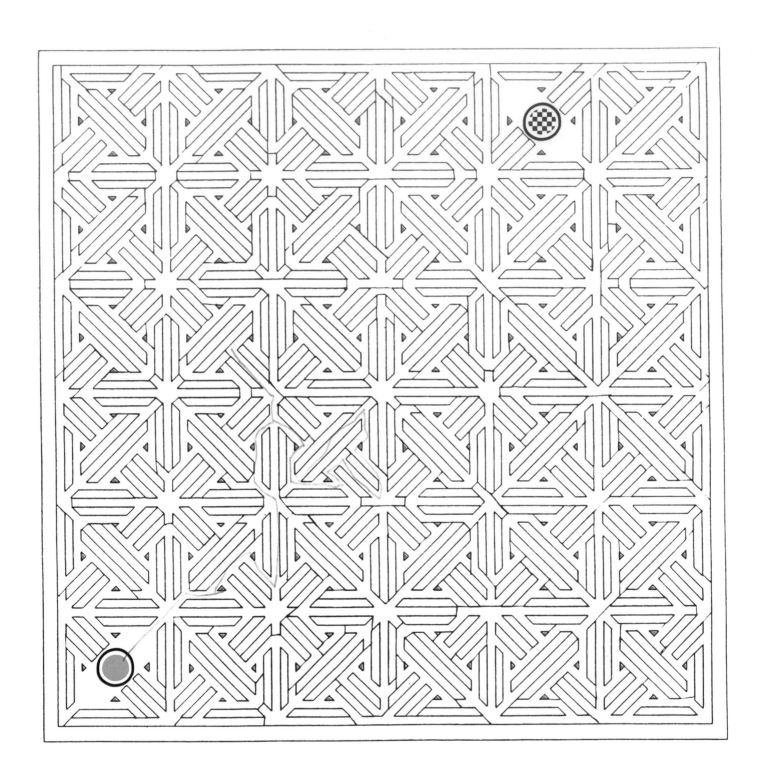

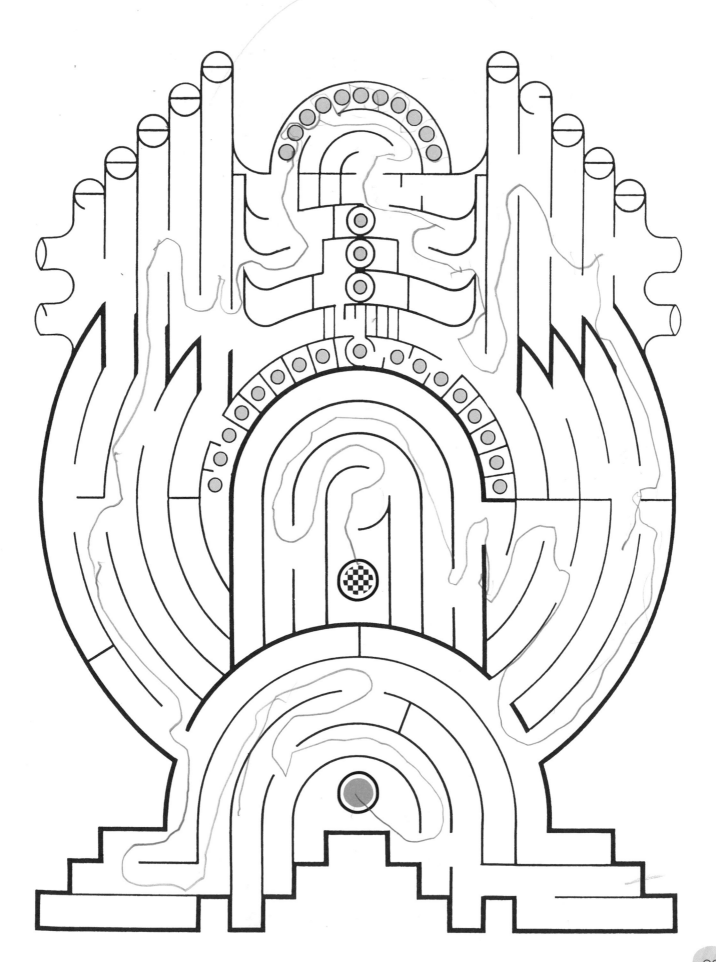

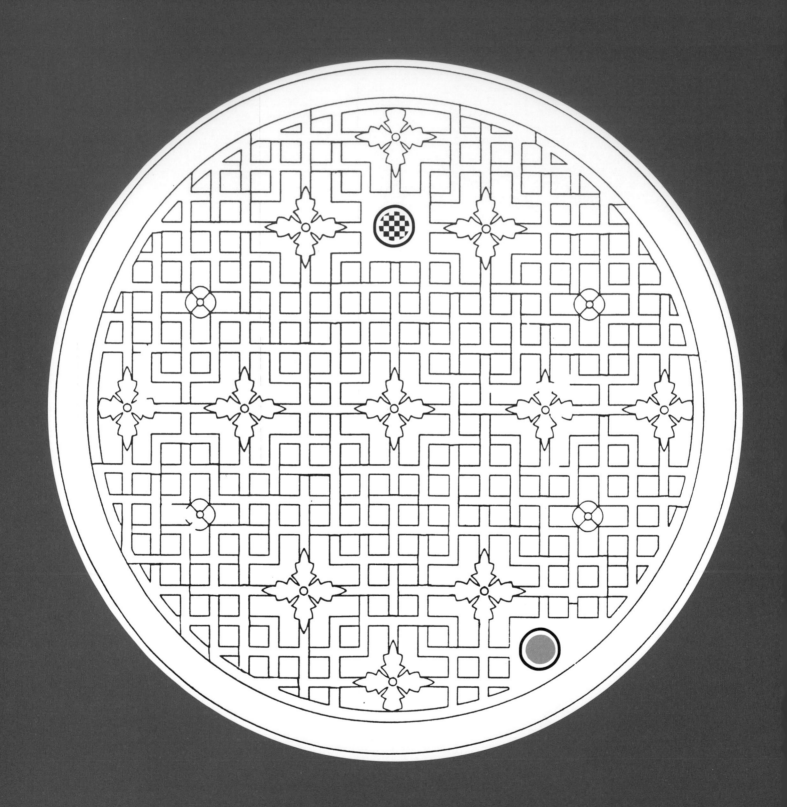

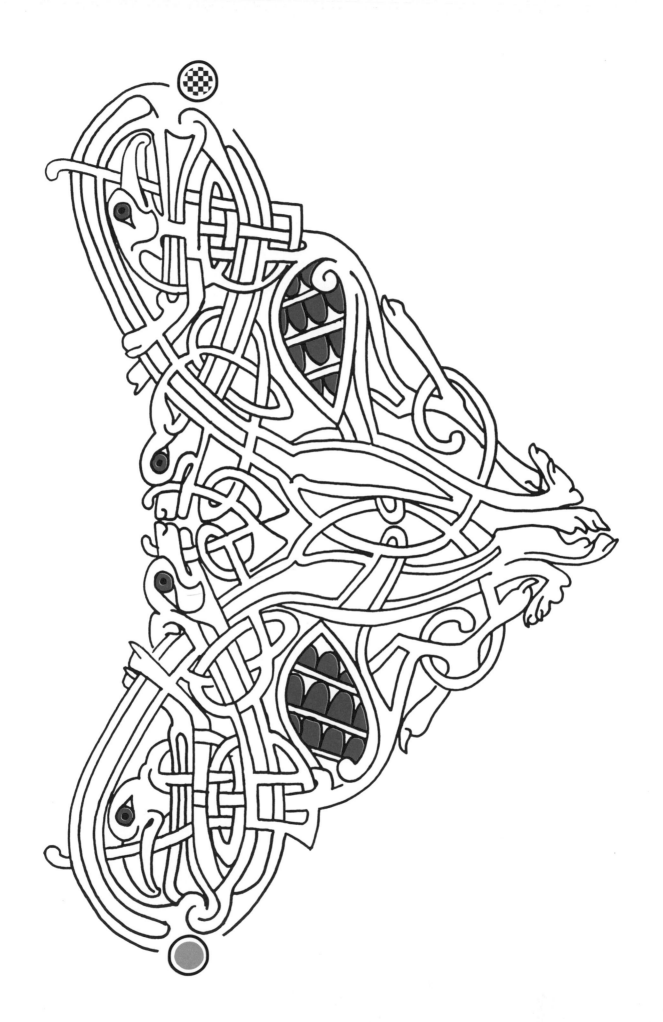

44

47

48

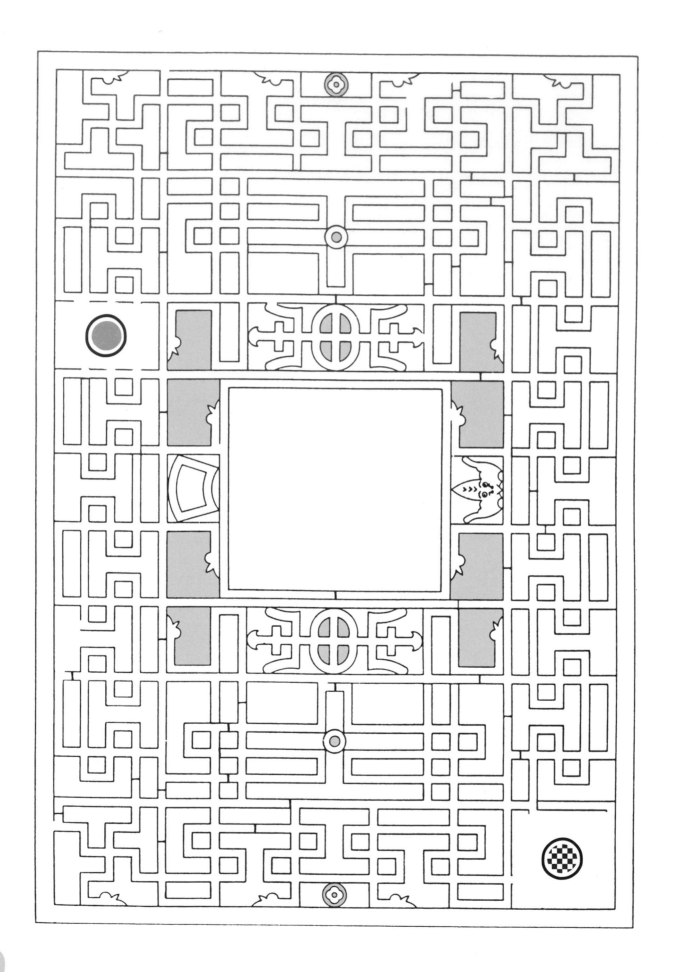

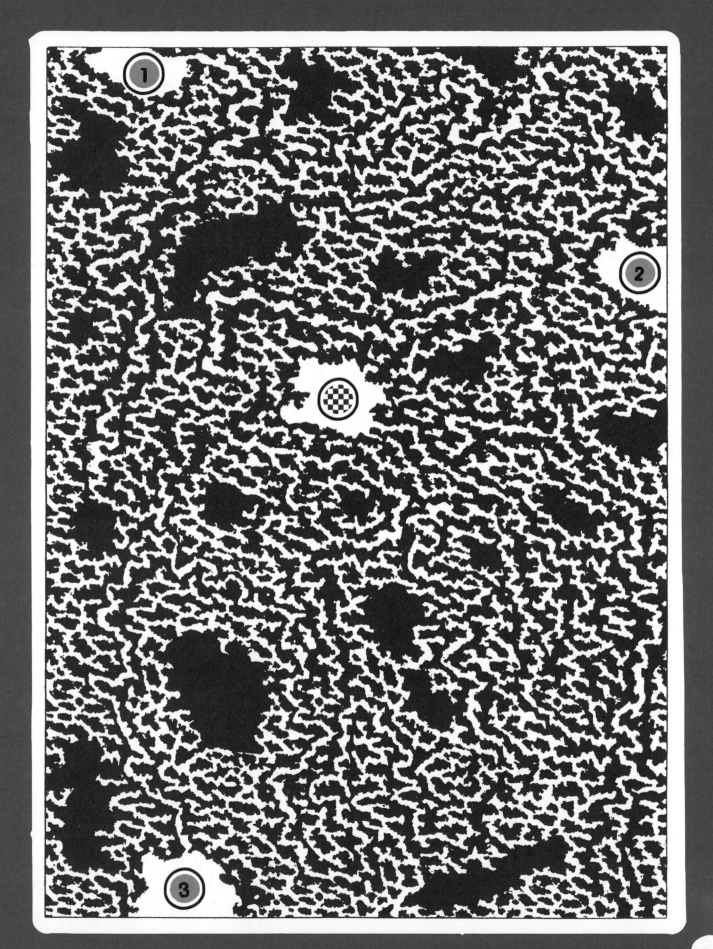

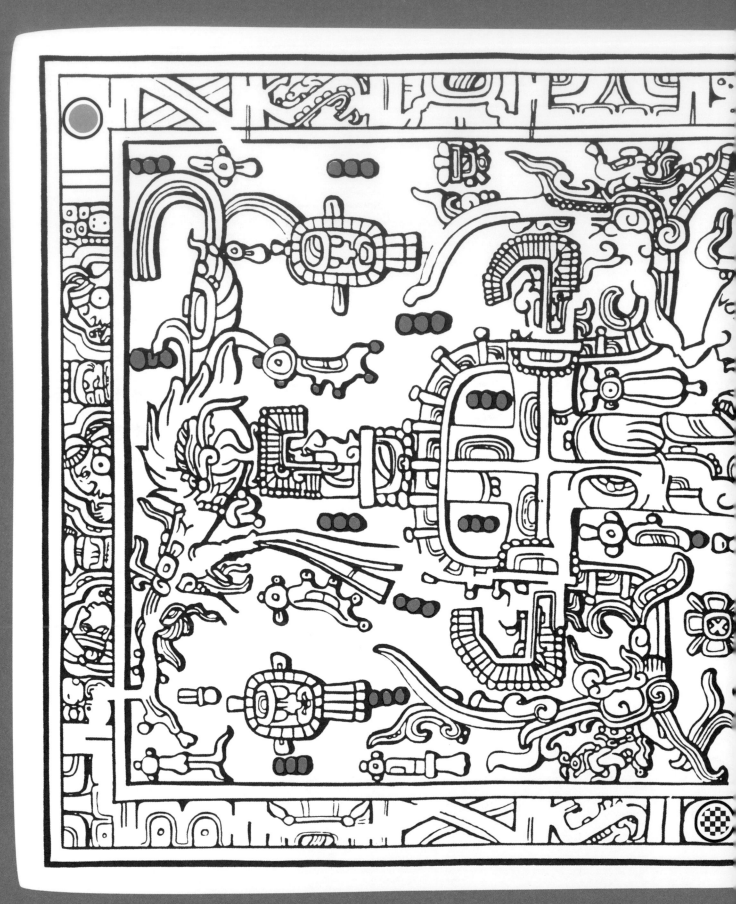

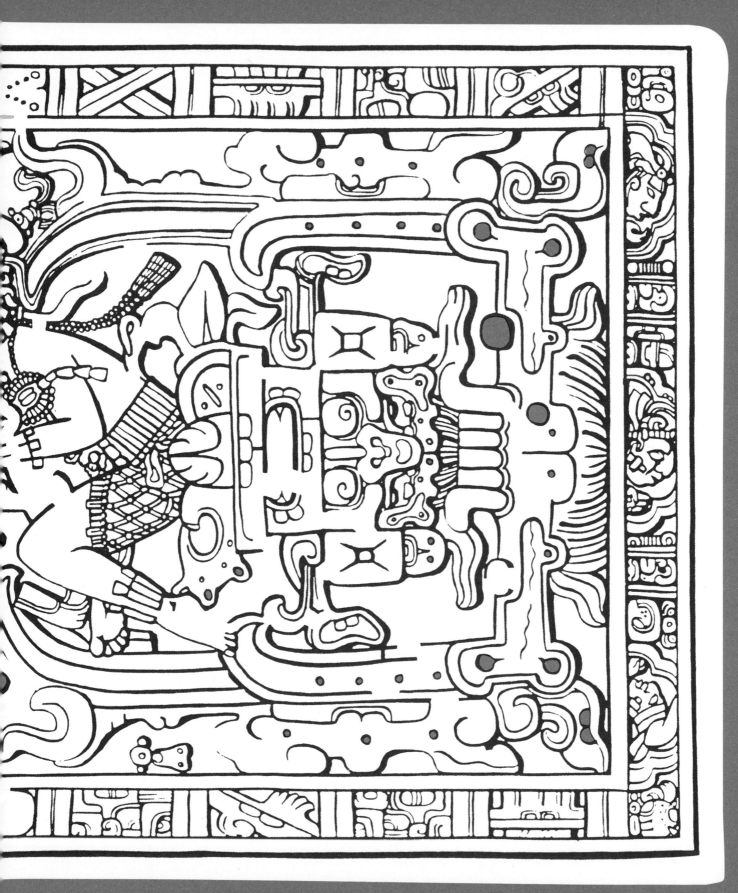

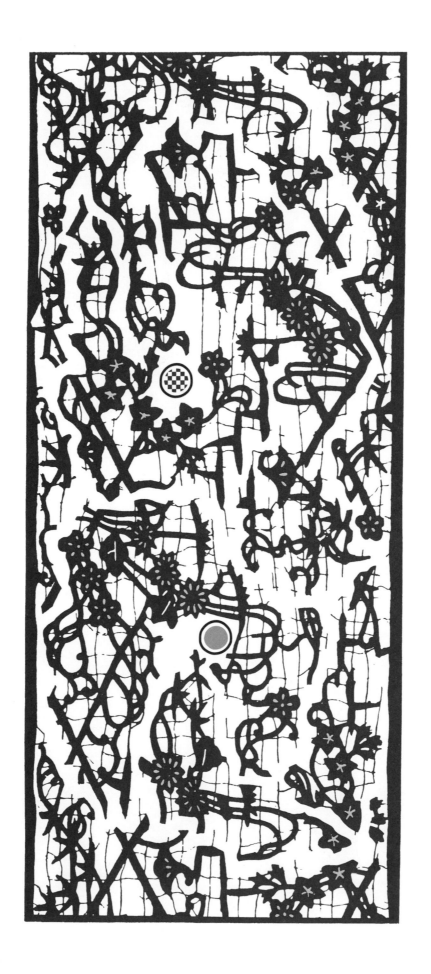

65

69

77

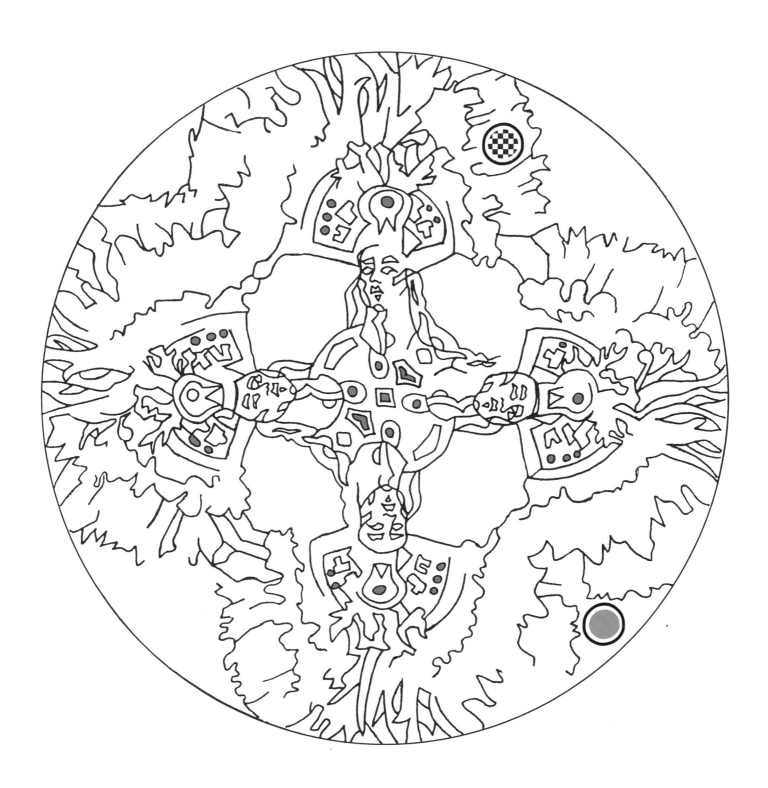

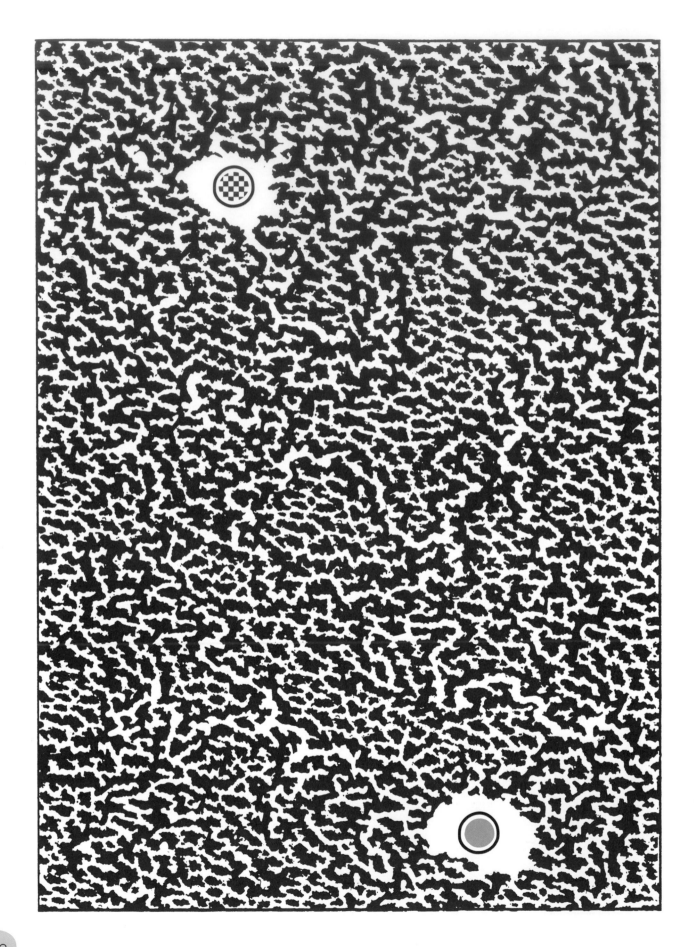

ANSWERS

7

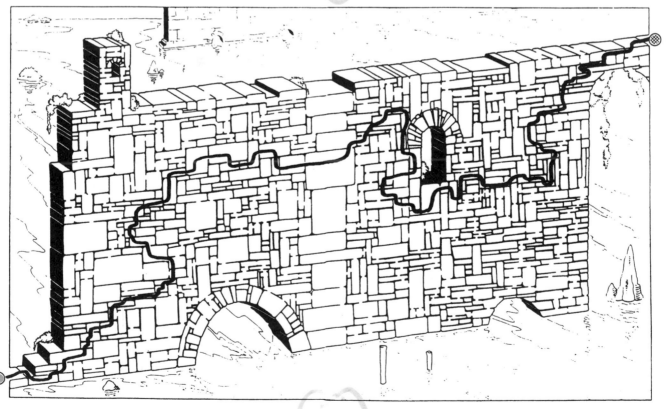

8-9

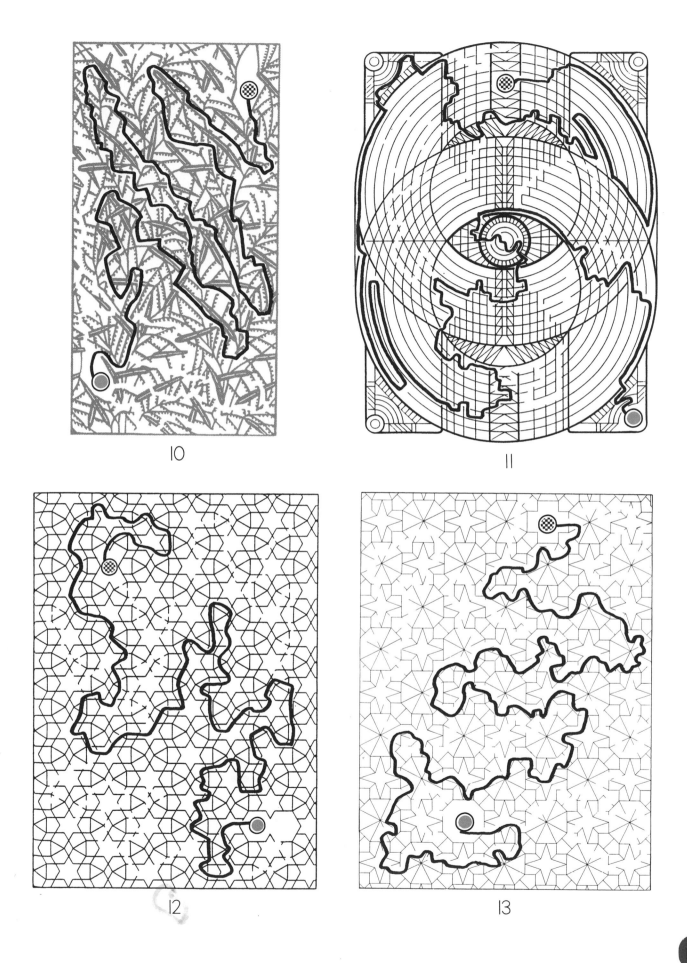

10

11

12

13

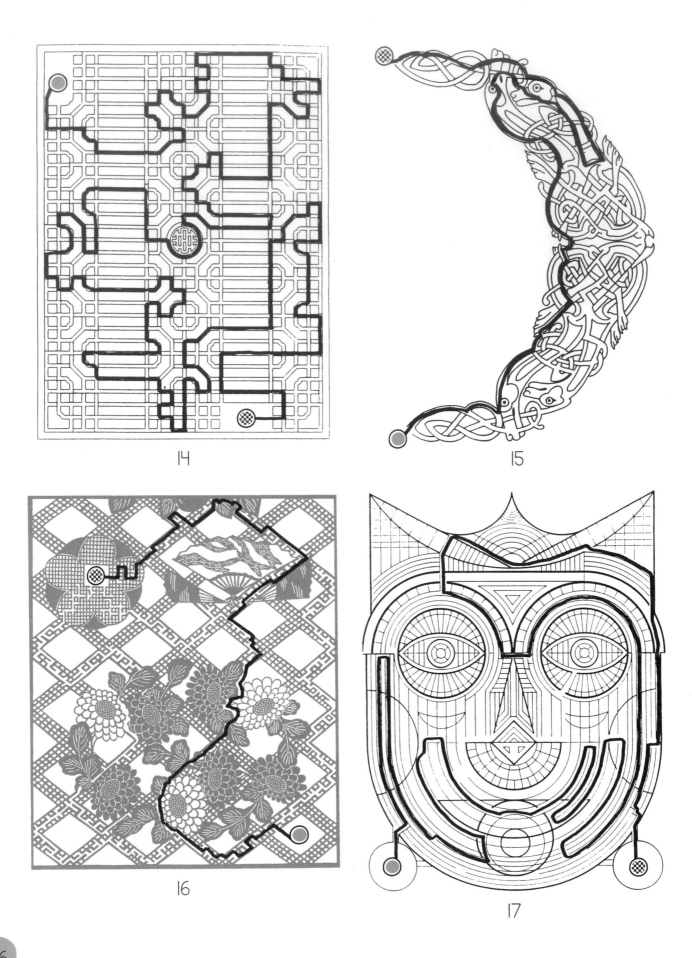

14

15

16

17

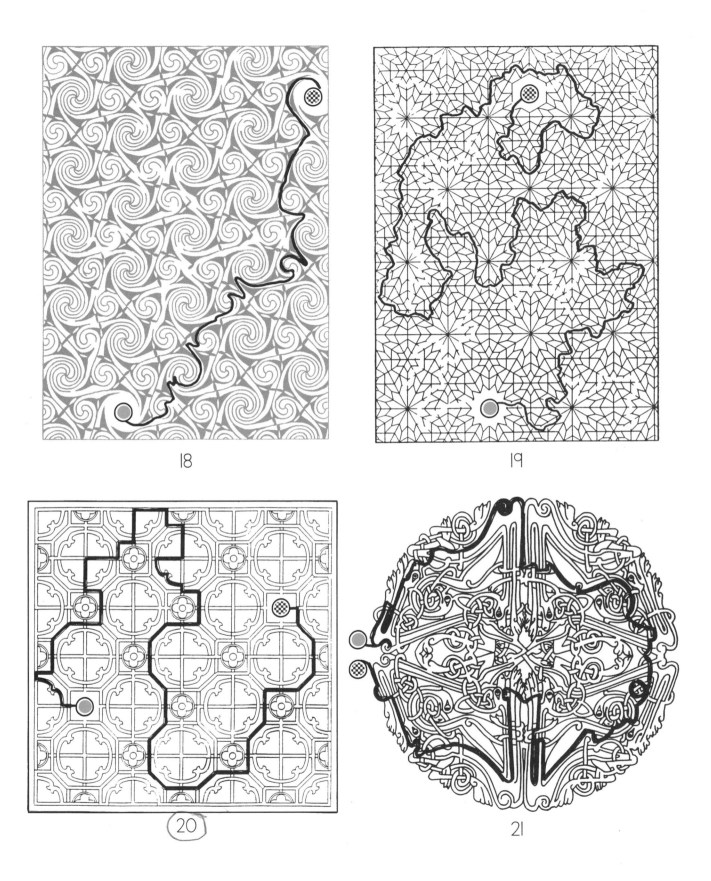

18

19

20

21

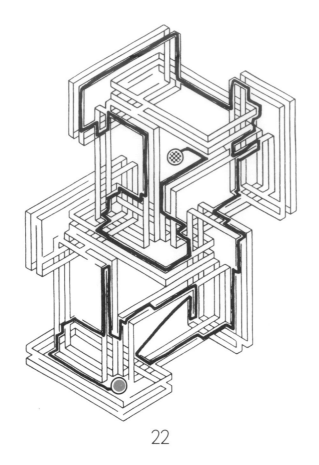

22

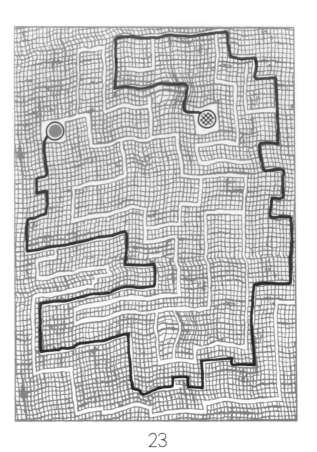

23

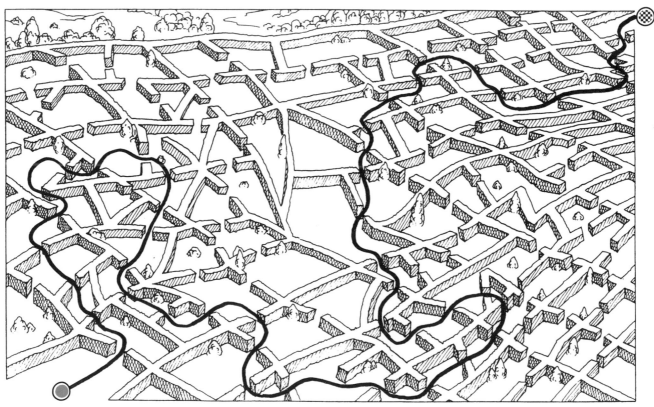

24-25

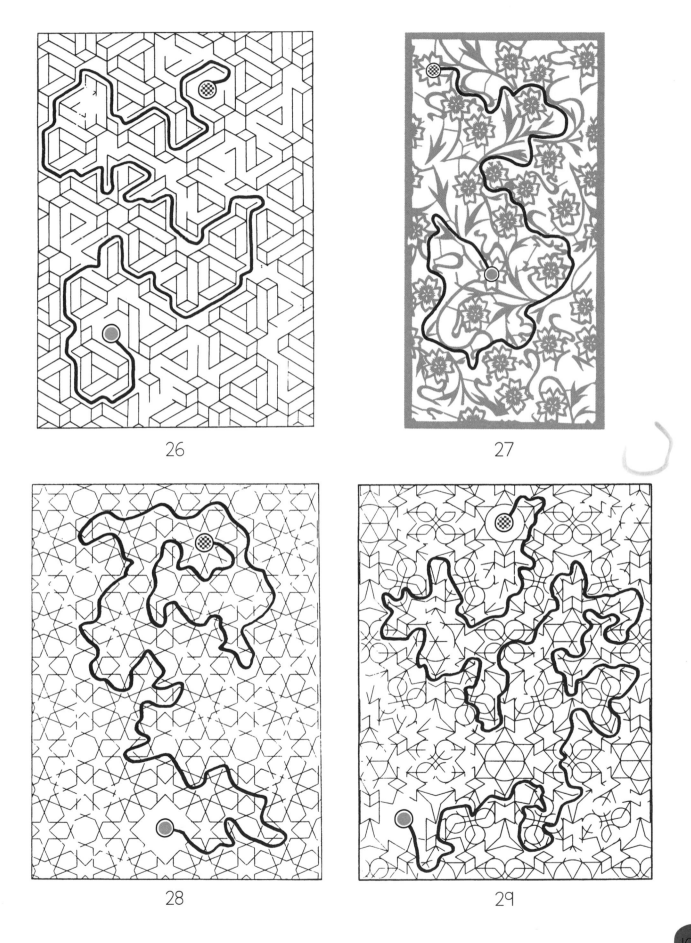

26

27

28

29

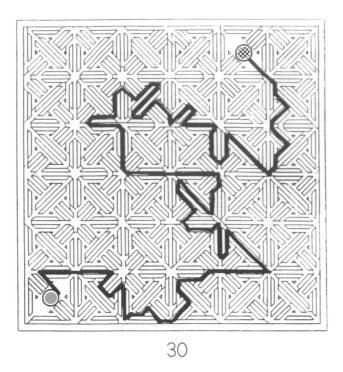

30

31

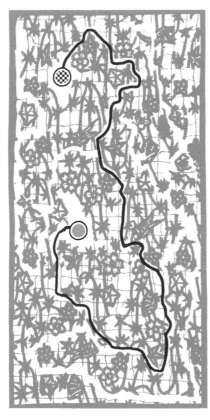

32

33

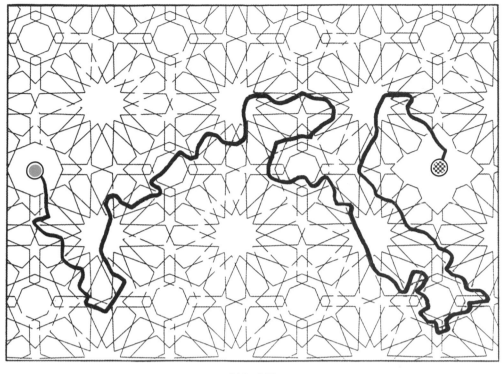

34-35

36

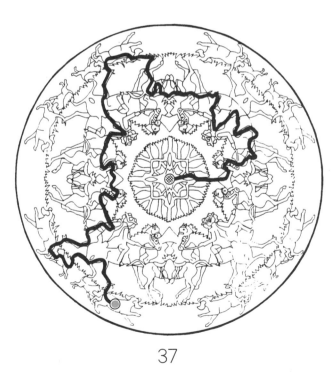

37

38

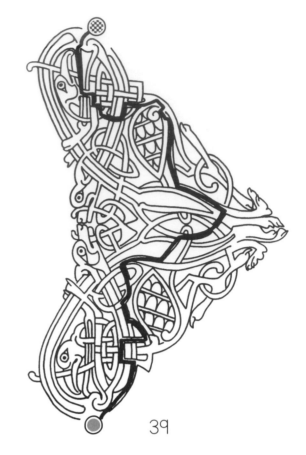

39

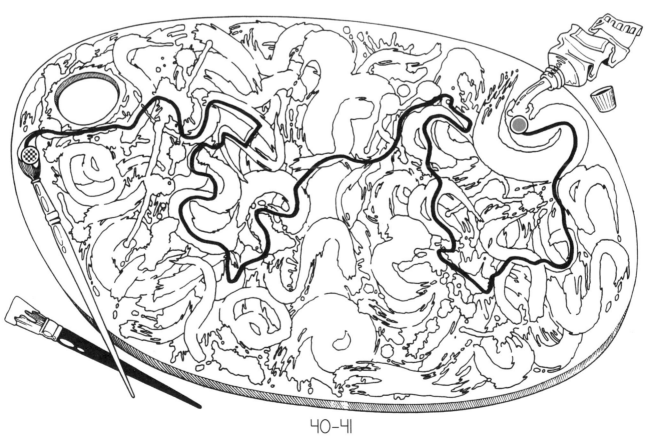

40-41

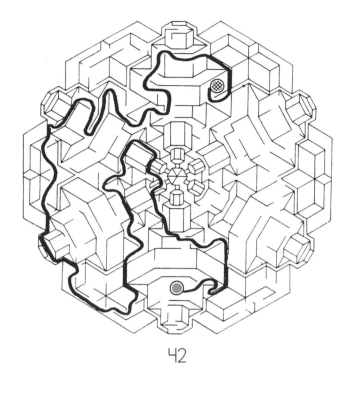

42

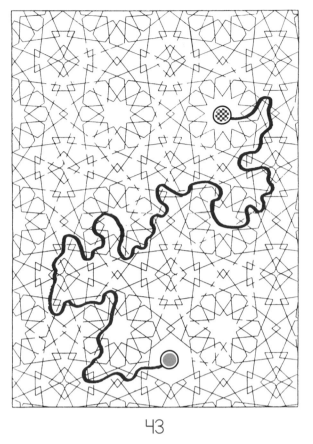

43

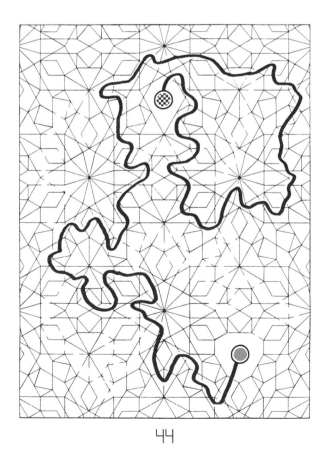

44

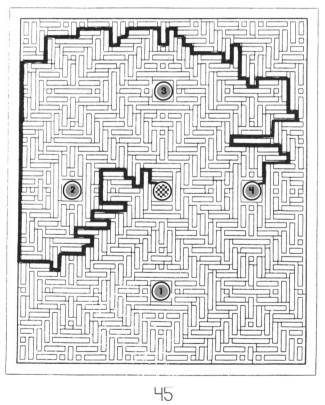

45

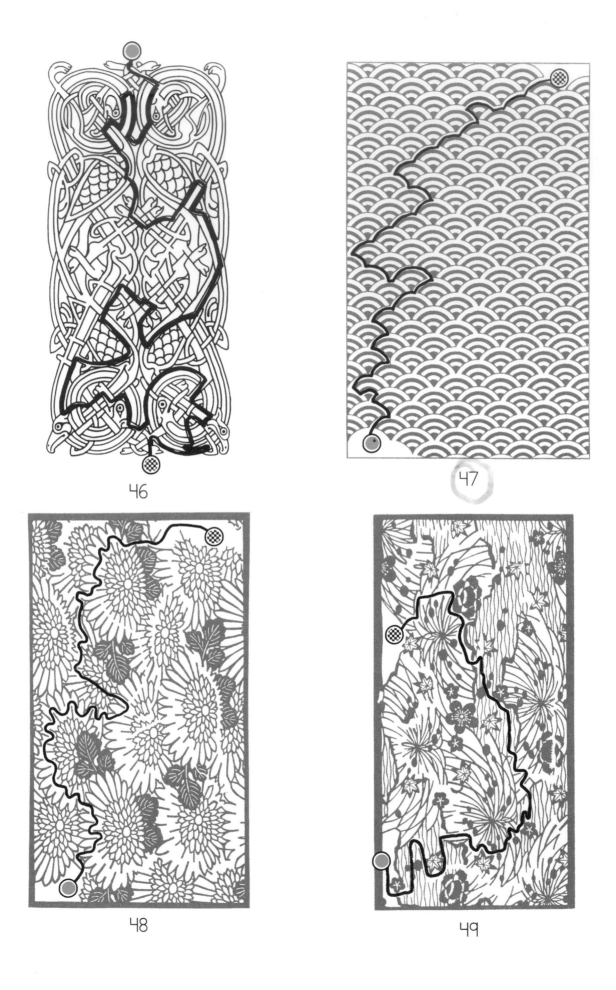

46

47

48

49

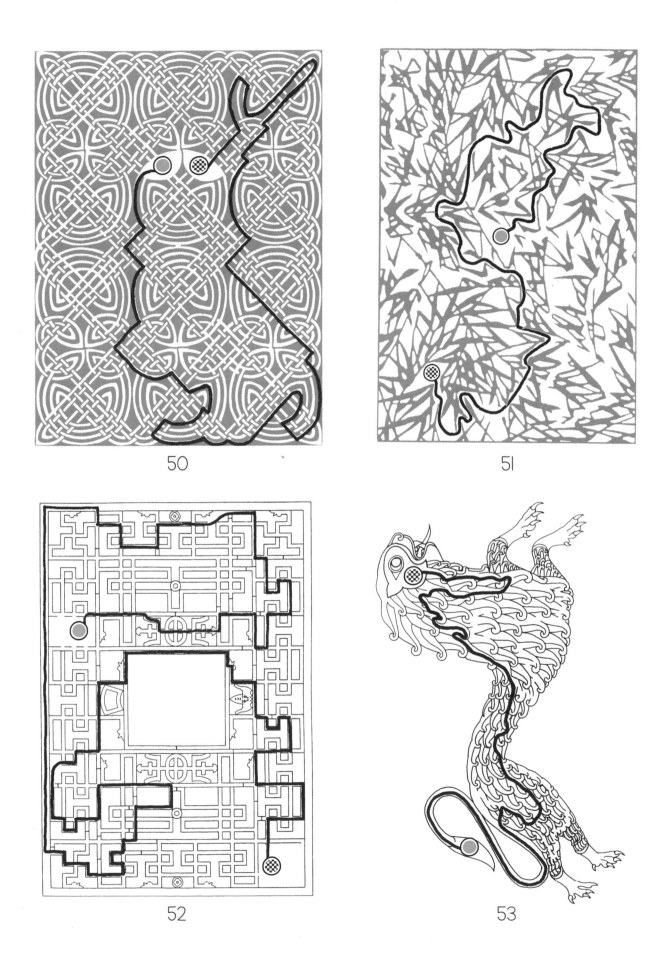

50

51

52

53

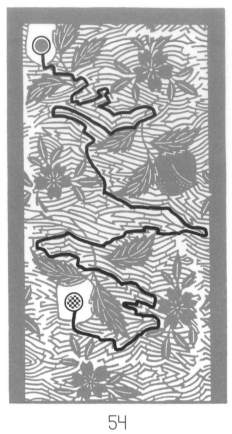

54

55

56-57

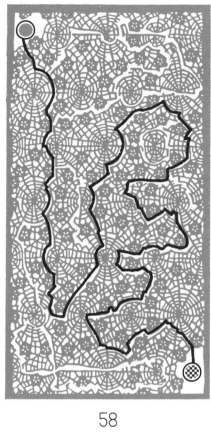

58

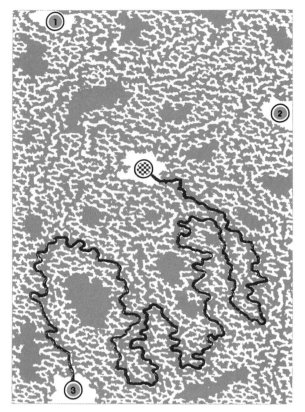

59

60–61

62

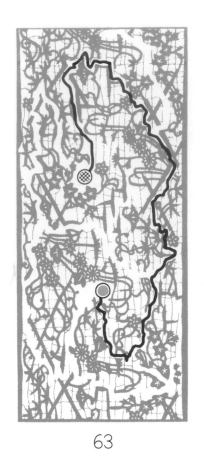

63

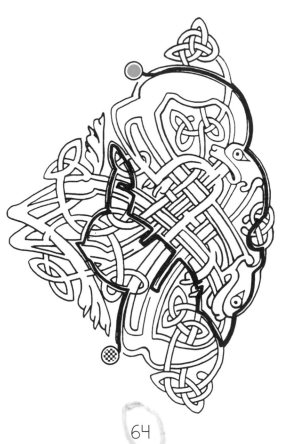

64

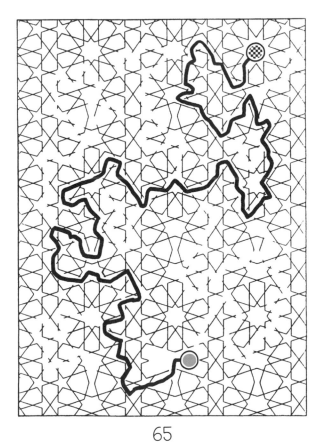

65

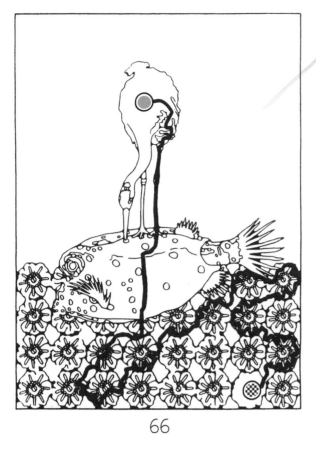

66

67

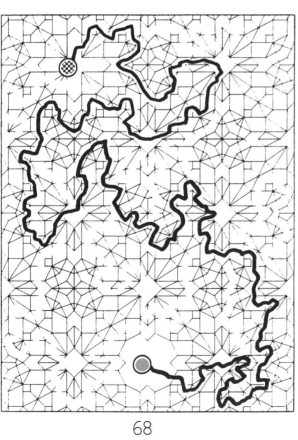

68

69

70-71

72

73

74

75

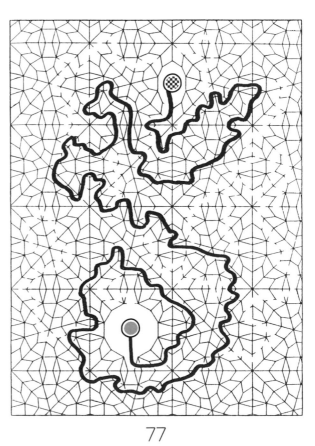

76

77

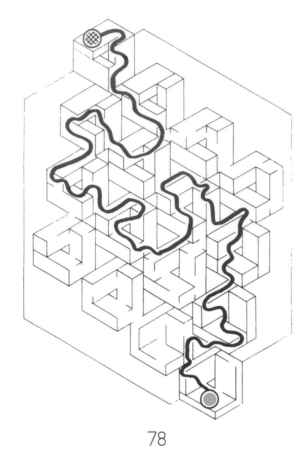

78

79

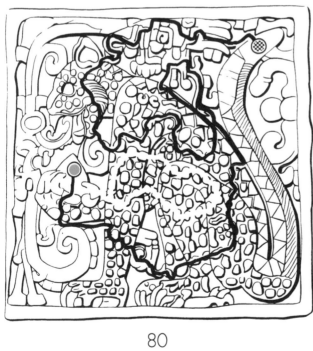

80

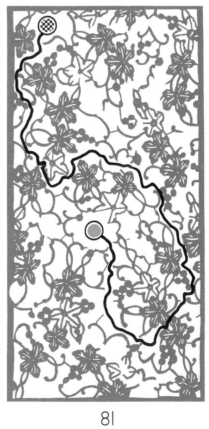

81

82

83

84-85

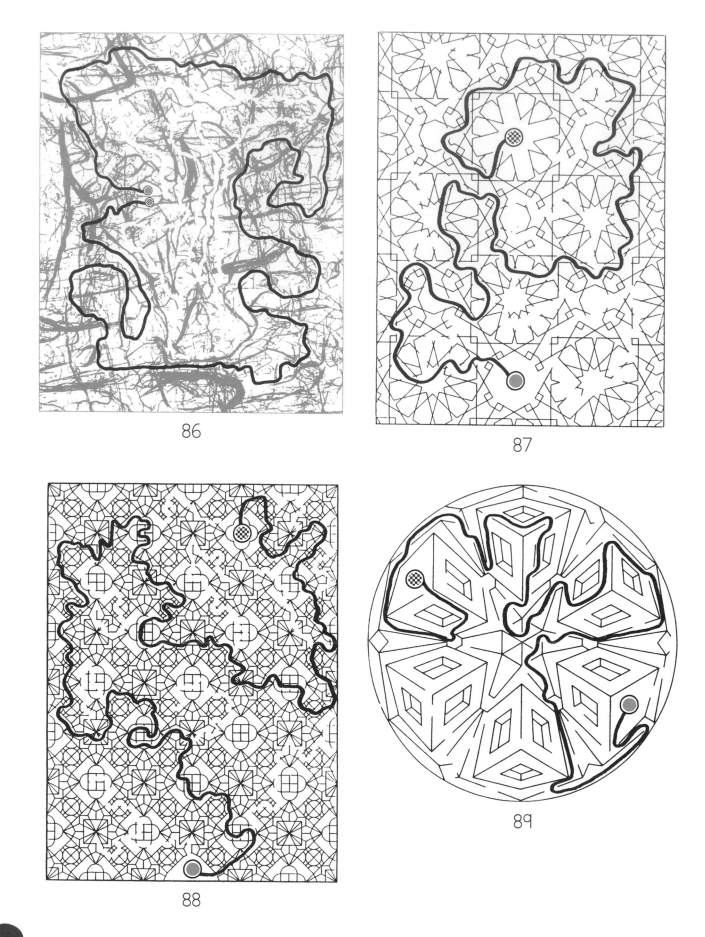

86

87

88

89

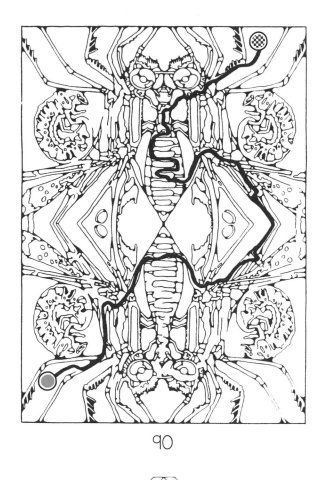

90

91

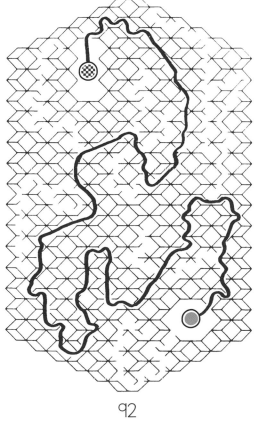

92

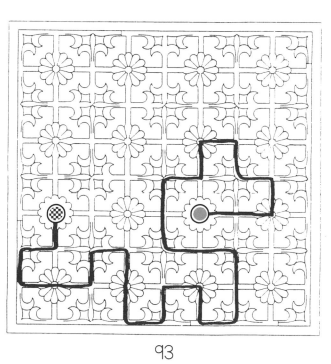

93

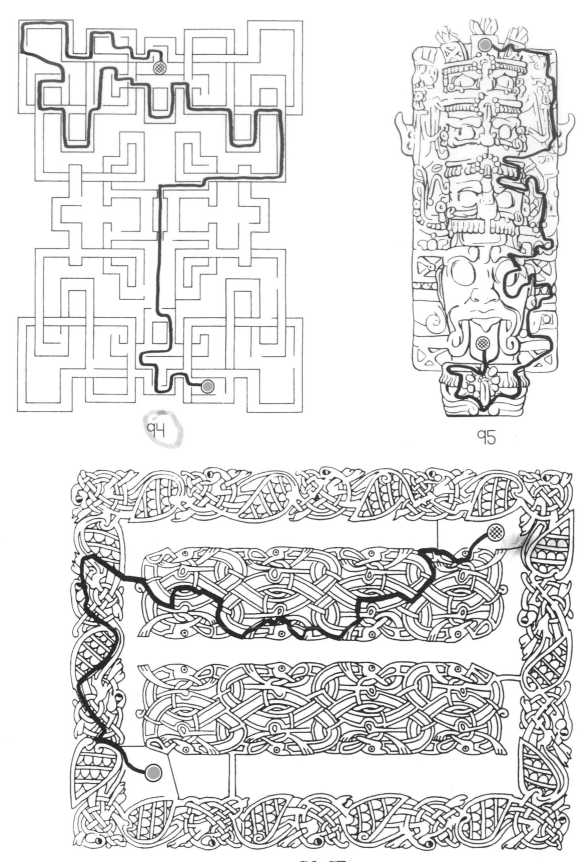

94

95

96-97

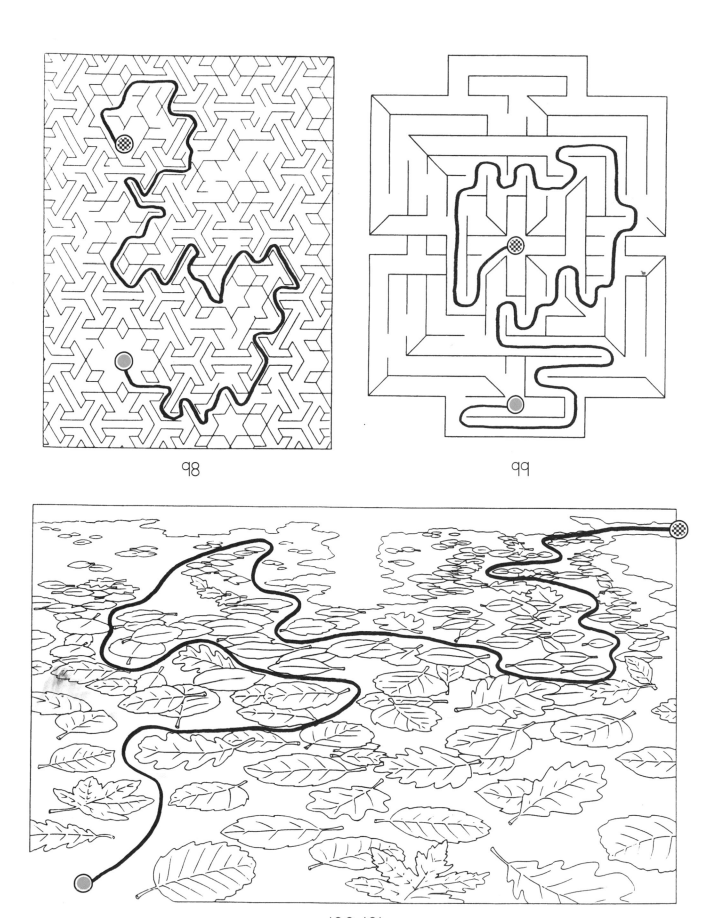

98

99

100-101

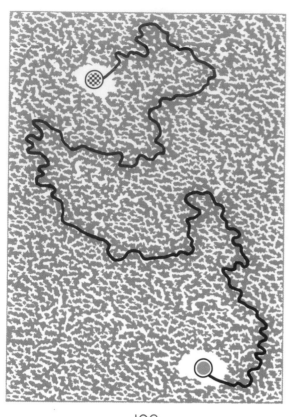

102

103